The Asce[illegible] Flame of Purification and Immortality

Initiations, Ceremonies and Prayers

The Ascension Flame of
Purification and Immortality

ISBN 978-0-9700902-9-4

English Publication - June 2007
Sixth Printing - June 2020

Mount Shasta Light Publishing
PO Box 1509
Mount Shasta CA 96067-1509
USA

Phone: 530-926-4599
Fax: 530-926-4159

mslpublishing.com
lemurianconnection.com

Front Cover Graphic of Lord Serapis Bey:
Marius Michael-George
MariusFineArt.com

Cover Design: Aaron Rose
Page Layout and Formatting: Aaron Rose

Printed in the USA

Table of Contents

Introduction

By Adama of Telos

This Ascension booklet, along with the Prayer booklet, are created and offered in print form to you and to the public at the request of the Masters of the Spiritual Hierarchy of our planet, including Lord Maitreya, the planetary Christ. In fact, both booklets are designed to be companion tools to the hard-cover book *The Seven Sacred Flames.*

A certain portion, less than half, of the information and prayers contained in the Ascension and the Prayer booklets has already been printed in the Seven Sacred Flames book. Nevertheless, we, the Masters of Wisdom in charge of this planetary evolution, wish to see a portion of that information mentioned again in these two booklets with added new information not mentioned in the other publications. It will be most important for those coming in contact with the booklets first.

The concept of the Ascension booklet came into being at the request of hundreds of people world-wide to have such a tool to be able to share what they have learned through reading the Telos books and taking the workshops we have sponsored through Aurelia. They requested to have something inexpensive in print they could easily carry with them and share with others. The booklets are created mainly, but not exclusively, for those coming in contact with our teachings who seriously wish to engage themselves in planetary service and Ascension. Use them as tools to assist in the creation of webs of Light everywhere on the planet, for self healing, the healing of humanity and of the Earth.

Your prayers and ceremonies will contribute to the purification and raising of your vibration and consciousness through individual and group activities. Each time you will engage your energies in that service, you will accelerate your own pathway and Ascension process. You will be joining energetically, as points of contacts and light, with others on the planet who are doing the same. You will be contributing to the expansion and the manifestation of the "momentum" that is required to literally lift the Earth and Her people into a fifth-dimensional frequency. It simply cannot happen without your active participation.

As Master Saint Germain gave the teaching a while back, he said:

> *Each time you pray for the Earth, the planet and others by sending Love and Light into dark or challenging situations, you are contributing to create a better world to live in. By doing so, you receive back the multiplication of the energies you sent out with an added 80% of what you have invoked. It is used for your own healing, advancement and acceleration. Your devotion to invoking the magical energies of the Seven Sacred Flames creates a win-win outcome for everyone, including the masters who consecrate their time, love and energy in assisting the evolution of every soul on this planet. We always join you in your prayers and you then become a team with Us.*

We invite you to acquire several copies of these booklets and share them freely with those you feel will receive them with an open heart. Get together with other like-minded people to do Ascension Ceremonies once or twice a month in your home or elsewhere. Also open your heart to create time to invoke the energies of the Sacred Fire through the prayers that are presented to you. When you do, ask us to join you and to multiply your efforts a thousand times. This kind of planetary service is part of your initiatic pathway and is required for those considering themselves candidates for Ascension.

Lord Serapis Bey

The Ascension Flame

of Purification and Immortality

Main God qualities and actions of the Fourth Ray:
Purity, wholeness, Christ consciousness and becoming God through the consciousness of the Divine Mother.

Corresponding Chakra: Base of the Spine
Color: Pure Dazzling White
Corresponding Stones: Azurite, Snow quartz and Mother of Pearl

Chohan of the Fourth Ray:
Lord Serapis Bey
His Retreat: The Great Hall of Ascension Temple at Luxor, Egypt

Archangels of the Fourth Ray with Divine Complement:
Gabriel and Hope
Their Retreat: Between Sacramento and Mount Shasta, CA, USA

Elohim of the Fourth Ray with Divine Complement:
Purity and Astrea
Their Retreat: Near Gulf of Archangels, Russia

About Lord Serapis Bey

Lord Serapis Bey is Chohan of the Fourth Ray, guardian of the Ascension Flame. He is the disciplinarian, known through the centuries for his strict discipline. Real discipline is not control over another to thwart innate progress, but instead holds in check the human qualities to allow the Real Self to have expression. This is essential for the attainment of Ascension which is the culmination of all embodiments. He is devoted to the perfection of the soul through compassion, patience, understanding and self-discipline. He assists all who call upon him in the development of the intuitive and creative faculties of the heart. Lord Serapis Bey can be called upon to open your eyes to the beauty of God's creations. He assists all who call upon him in expressing their most heart-felt creative aspects.

Embodiments of Lord Serapis Bey

- Serapis Bey was embodied as a high priest in the Ascension Temple on Atlantis more than 11,500 years ago. He is the one who brought the Ascension Flame from Atlantis to Egypt just prior to the destruction of that continent.
- Serapis Bey spent many lifetimes along the Nile, and as the Egyptian pharaoh Amenhotep III (1417-1379 BC), he was called "the Magnificent." He brought Egypt to the height of diplomatic prestige, prosperity and peace. His extensive building of monuments, palaces and temples included construction of the Temple of Luxor.
- His most familiar incarnation was Leonidas, King of Sparta, the great warrior who led the Spartans in the famous battle at Thermopylae, Greece.
- Serapis Bey ascended around 400 B.C.

The Temple of Luxor

In the land of Egypt, along the banks of the Nile River, there exists the focus of the Great White Brotherhood dedicated to preserving the Cosmic Flame of Ascension. The Ascension Temple at Luxor sustains the pulsation of the Ascension Flame in the atmosphere of Earth. Those of the human race who awaken in each century with the desire to complete the cycles of incarnation become the responsibility of the Ascension Brotherhood. Their service to Life is to create the opportunity of necessary initiations for the neophytes who come to Luxor to qualify for Ascension. Serapis Bey, Lord of Love, explains that Luxor provides the opportunity for spiritual development.

The Ascension Flame at Luxor, and the one generated in Telos, both hold the same frequencies and are available for the people of Earth. This flame is utilized freely by the nature kingdom in its resurrection each successive season of spring.

From Lord Serapis Bey: ***The candidate for Ascension must meet "seven major initiations." The candidate must successfully pass through the disciplines of the Seven Great Temples.***

"I am embodied discipline," says Serapis Bey. For centuries most people have feared that discipline. I am dedicated to seeing that you pass through the fires of purification, and that you, who desire the opportunity of gaining your ascension, might persevere until the day of that victory. Angels of the Ascension Temple gather all the praise, adoration, songs, devotion and blessings sent upward by individuals in congregational or individual worship. These energies created by devotional practices are carefully woven into the ever-widening spiritual stream of energy. Each new soul who attains Ascension status makes it easier for the next lifestream to avail itself of the fully-gathered cosmic momentum of those who have gone before.

First: The candidate must learn to control and transform all thoughts and feelings that are not aligned with their Divine Self. This is the initiation of mastery of the first temple, the Temple of God's Will, that the hopeful and the brave must pass. The candidate must learn to commune with his own God Presence and to develop within himself true humility before it. Within this first temple, under the direction of Master El Morya and his assistants, the aspirant is assisted in the dissolving of rebellion. Rebellion took Lucifer from the heart of heaven; the rebellion against discipline and self-correction is a barrier to real spiritual progress. Within the discipline of a good night's sleep, abstinence from tobacco, alcohol and recreational drugs, you ease your pathway to your glorious freedom. Those who do not wish to accept those disciplines have not yet the stimulus to become the best, to be the highest and the greatest expression of a God incarnate.

Second: Those who have successfully passed the initiations of the first temple are taken to the second temple, known as the Temple of Learning. Under the guidance of Lord Lanto, Master Kuthumi and the Brotherhood of the Golden Robe, they are given instructions in the Law. Here they develop understanding of the Law of cause and effect and all other Universal Laws. It is a pleasant and happy time of sowing the seeds, of breathing life upon those seeds and bringing in a harvest of work. It is the time when the artist develops his skills, the musician develops dexterity in his musical accomplishments and the teacher becomes eloquent in conveying knowledge to his students.

Third: Those who have successfully passed the initiations of the second temple are taken to the third temple, the Temple of Love, under the great protection and guidance of the Beloved Paul the Venetian. Here the neophyte must learn the discipline of unconditional love and harmony for their own lifestream and for all other forms of Life. They are placed in living quarters with those who have within themselves tendencies which are particularly aggravating to others. This is where the numbers of neophytes dwindle, and with great feeling of relief, many candidates rush to the door and leave us. To live peacefully with one's fellowmen is one of the greatest tests of the unascended state. Although the graciousness, the beauty, the kindliness of this great Master are so astonishing as to melt a heart of stone, the discipline he requires in learning tolerance, compassion and understanding is such that few survive.

Fourth: From the third temple, the initiate moves into the fourth temple, the Temple of Ascension. This is the first personal contact that Serapis Bey has with the neophyte. For the first time, the candidate must draw forth enough purity to see his I AM Presence and his Holy Christ Self face-to-face. In the initiation, the Master himself will stand within the aura of the initiate, presenting many imbalances which still exist within the inner bodies. This is when the candidate will hear many voices and only true discrimination, prayer, selflessness and humility can discern the "Voice of the Silence." It is the time when the "Self" is shown the tricks of the ego and subtle appearances. The aspirant must apply himself to purify all past negative human creations and transform them into pure-white Light Radiance.

Fifth: After passing the initiation of the fourth temple, disciples are ready for the discipline of the fifth temple, the Temple of Consecration. It is then that the garment of consecration is placed upon them, golden sandals on their feet and a silken robe on their body. Master Hilarion or Beloved Raphael performs the service of consecration where all body systems are consecrated to purity and ascension. Then consecrations are given, of the hands into which the Flame of Healing is infused, and of the feet which become the anchors of the Sacred Fire wherever the body moves. Consecration of the lips takes place to speak the Sacred Words which invoke and command the manifestation of precipitation and healing powers. Consecration of the energies of the eyes enables the disciple to see perfection and to call it forth. This completes the consecrations.

Sixth: The aspirant is then taken to the sixth temple, the Temple of Service, where he is expected to temporarily put aside his worldly pursuits to be in service to others and to become his brother's keeper. He is also expected to volunteer some of his time to planetary service for the benefit of mankind, not just for himself and his family. He must learn to include the rest of humanity in his heart, becoming fully aware that the needs of others also affect the needs of many. In the sixth temple, under the sponsorship of Lord Sananda with his beloved twin flame Nada *(also known as Jesus and Mary Magdalene),* the aspirant is trained to nurture and serve all aspects of Life and become a ministering servant.

Before a candidate for ascension can become a master, he must also learn the disciplines of the humble servant, selfless service, true brotherhood and obedience to Hierarchy. Those spending almost their entire lives in the service of some activity or organization to assist and enhance the consciousness of the collective are usually sixth level initiates. In the past, too often, Serapis Bey saw many of you leave Luxor, ready to set the world on fire, only to recede back as you went down the steps of the great temple. This is where a great number of you lost your opportunity for Ascension in many incarnations.

Seventh: After the aspirant passes the initiations of the first six temples, he is ready to enter the seventh temple, the Temple of the Violet Fire where every atom, cell and electron of his being becomes completely purified by the action of the Violet Flame under the sponsorship of Master Saint Germain. The candidate becomes like a window through which the God-life flows with absolute purity. The physical body will give you the greatest possible ease and grace within the Laws of harmony, if you refrain from taking into the physical body those substances which change its natural vibratory action, disconnecting it from the harmony of the spheres of Divine Love. When the candidate is ready to fully externalize the Will of God, and preparations begin to initiate the final phase of the graduation ceremony of Ascension, then all is in place for the candidate to become an "ascended master." Do you see? Blessings from the heart of Luxor!

Transmission from the Heart of Lord Serapis Bey, the Lord of Love

Beloved Brothers and Sisters of Earth, with the great Love of my Heart, I send to each one who reads this material the blessings of Luxor and of Telos. Realize, beloved ones, that never in the history of the Earth, has the opportunity for humanity to attain the freedom of their glorious Ascension been offered with so much ease and grace in this wondrous time of preparation for your planet's Ascension. An exceptional window of opportunity is presented to those of humanity who wish to gain their spiritual freedom and who are willing to do whatever it takes to make it happen.

I am not proclaiming that it will be entirely easy for everyone. My promise to you is that I, and the large teams of the Ascension Brotherhood of Luxor and of Telos, stand ready to support and coach, with much love and compassion, those who will seriously commit to their evolution. Yes, many of you will face temporary challenges from time to time, but if you face them with surrender, devotion, joy, enthusiasm, and the attitude of gratitude for the exceptional opportunity offered to you at this time, be assured that the rest of your path does not have to be difficult.

It all has to do with the perceptions and reactions you feel regarding what presents itself in your life as an opportunity to align past karma and integrate the lessons you need to learn in order to become an Ascended Master. Though the initiations are basically the same for everyone, they manifest in a different way for each lifestream according to the unique pathway and one's own level of initiation and evolution.

Know, beloved ones, that once you have made a serious commitment to your Ascension, all heaven is at your beck and call to assist you in a most wondrous way. In former times, the Ascension was extremely difficult to attain. With the new dispensation now given to humanity by your Creator, the pathway basically remains the same, but you now have so much more assistance available to you and so much more information that those in the past did not have access to.

Luxor and Telos are waiting for your return. Most of you have come to both places many times, but many of you left, fearing that it would be too difficult. And you are still here on the surface of Earth, often in pain and despair. Realize that the temporary difficulties on the path are so much easier to bear than the lifetimes of pain and struggle you experienced once you embraced the illusion that you could not do it.

In fact, I say to all of you that if you are really serious about ascending in this life and if you apply all the Laws of Love with absolute constancy and perseverance, "you can do it." With our help and with the help of your "I AM Presence" and your "Higher Mental Body," nothing is impossible. In fact, it is not only possible but most desirable for your evolution that you do not stay behind in the third dimension very long after the Earth's Ascension around 2012. This is my promise to you that we will match your efforts in assisting each one of you. We love you all very dearly and our dedication to assist you is so absolute! Once you discover the real truth about Ascension, you will no longer hesitate to let go of the outmoded lifestyles you have accepted as "normal," and prepare yourself to live as a true Child of God.

On behalf of those of the Ascension Brotherhood of Luxor who serve with me in the Holy Purpose of holding the Sacred Energies of the Ascension Flame, we send to all of you who read our words of Wisdom, our deepest Love and Mantle of Peace. I AM Serapis Bey from the Ascension Temple of Luxor!

Discourse from Adama with Serapis Bey

Peace and love from the Heart of Lemuria, this is Adama with the Chohan of the Fourth Ray, our beloved Serapis Bey. I bring you the blessings of my Light and the victory that lies within it. We are bidding you our most heartfelt welcome.

Lord Serapis Bey came today with his team of masters, known as "The Ascension Brotherhood of Luxor," who specialize in this service. These masters extend to you now the elixir of their heart's love through the purifying fires of the Ascension Flame. Breathe this in, my beloveds; this is a gift to you. These dedicated beings have worked closely with our brother Serapis Bey for several centuries, planning the evolution of the human race for the time that has finally come. Their service to Life consists of the engagement of their energies in preparing for the uplifting of our planet and the consciousness of humanity for planetary ascension in the years to come.

The Ascension Temple at Luxor sustains the pulsation of the Ascension Flame in the atmosphere of Earth, as does our Ascension Temple in Telos. Visualize two temples, united in consciousness and in energy, blessing and loving daily and hourly everything on Earth for the benefit of ascending humanity. With each successive spring season, this Sacred Flame is freely and widely utilized by the beings of the nature kingdom to assist the renewal and resurrection of the beauty of Nature. Each soul on Earth desiring to complete their cycle of incarnations by the process of Ascension is placed under the tutelage of the Ascension Brotherhood and the Office of the Christ.

A couple of hundred years ago, a great portion of the activities and records that this great pyramid held for so long in Luxor was either transferred or duplicated in Telos. The relocation of records was implemented then, because the spiritual hierarchy of the planet could foresee future potential problems in that area of the globe. The records and energies of that sacred focus could not be compromised in the event of regional or global cataclysms on the horizon at that time. So now, Telos has become the main focus of Ascension for this planet in total union and cooperation with the great masters of Luxor. We all work together in perfect harmony for the benefit of the collective. This is one of the fifth dimensional protocols.

The decision was made that the records of this important planetary focus would be safer underground, and best guarded in their original purity and sacredness, nurtured and honored by a large number of ascended beings, such as those of us in Telos.

Although it may seem that there are now two main Ascension focuses on the planet, I say that for us, it is only one. In the dimension where we function, time and space, as most of you understand it, do not exist, and all is one.

After the sinking of Atlantis and Lemuria, the surface populations have continued to war against each other until this day. Keep up your hope and your courage, my beloveds. Know that it will not be tolerated much longer; this consciousness will soon come to an end and be healed.

In Telos, soon after the destruction of both continents, we volunteered for the task of keeping the Flame of Ascension on behalf of mankind as our service to this planet, in order to insure its continuity. From the Love of our Hearts, we extend to you this day your opportunity to embrace and expand this wondrous Flame within your hearts for your own Ascension. We say that the heart ascends first, and then the rest follows.

Aurelia - Will a large percentage of humanity ascend by 2012?

Adama - Although there is greater assistance offered to humanity than ever before in Earth's history, and the Ascension process is made easier than ever before, none of you will be lifted into the Ascension process until you have met all the requirements and reached this frequency in your consciousness, no matter how long it takes in the cycles of time.

It will be required of those aspiring for Ascension that you heal and transform all your erroneous belief systems and embrace love, harmlessness and the truth of your divinity. Realize that the year 2012 is not the end of the ascension cycle on this planet, but simply a wondrous beginning. The full planetary process for the Earth, in the completion of Her full glory and destiny is a 2,000-year plan. In 2012, it is the Earth, Herself, making her Ascension into the Light, along with those who have met all the necessary requirements.

In the years following 2012, all souls incarnated on Earth will continue their evolution and ascend only when they are ready at the soul level. For some it may take six months, others five to eight years and for many, it will be longer. You will need to engage yourself seriously in the initiation process leading to ascension. Each one's journey is unique, and though the initiatic process is similar for everyone, it unfolds differently for each soul, according to their own distinctive pathway.

Aurelia - *Adama, would you describe the Ascension Flame?*

Adama - This Flame contains the frequency and color of all the other Flames. You see or experience it as a brilliant, luminous, white dazzling light that consumes on contact all that is less than the perfection of Love. Its power and brilliance are limitless, sustaining worlds in perfect harmony and beauty.

Those invoking and working with it must prepare for change. Once touched by that Flame, you are never the same again. Everyone can work with it, of course, but in its full intensity, it holds the capacity to completely transform the initiate who has reached the doorway of Ascension. When you are finally ready to take this leap in your evolution, you will be immersed in the frequency of that magnificent energy. It will propel you into the final step, when the fires of Love will consume all human limitations, your full consciousness will be restored and all your bodies will align and unite. You will then be invited to join the "immortals" as an ascended master. You will step into that glorious spiritual freedom and consciously reconnect with your Creator and with all that exists within His heart. This is, my friends, how powerful the Ascension Flame is.

Aurelia - *How can we consciously reach and maintain this level of frequency?*

Adama - This information has been given to the people of Earth again and again, but it has been ignored; in this age, it is given again through a wide variety of writings and channelings. It has been presented to you in so many packages and colors that you fail to recognize it.

Unless a teaching and key of wisdom is learned thoroughly and integrated through the heart, it remains "just information" and clutter in your mind, soon forgotten. Ultimately, it does not advance the evolution of your consciousness. We know people who have read hundreds of spiritual books; they have acquired mental knowledge, but when this knowledge is not integrated to embody their divinity, spiritual progress remains marginal.

Allow me to mention to you briefly again, repeating what has been said before, in the hope that if repeated often enough, it will eventually sink in. "Ascension" does not require the doing of so many things, but is all about becoming, embracing and remembering to live your lives as the God/Goddess that you are. It means fully embracing the divinity that already exists within you through the expansion of your consciousness as Beings of Love, and living from the wisdom of the heart. It is that simple, my beloveds. If you become this, you do not need anything else. All this already exists and lives within you. I remind you that there is nothing outside the Self.

Here are some of the main points or guidelines to be understood and considered about the initiatic path leading to your graduation from Earth's curriculum through the Ascension protocols.

- This process is one of complete purification and healing of all that is hindering your transfiguration, resurrection and ascension into the arms of God/Love; the restoration of your dignity and memories, so that you live, once again, as divine children of your heavenly Father/Creator, entering the world of "Oneness."

- Understand that each dimension represents a certain frequency. The fifth dimension becomes accessible to you when, and only when, you have attained that frequency in your consciousness and have the ability to maintain it at all times.

- Live from the heart, talking and acting like a master would, as a way of "being." Always ask yourself the question, "What would a master do or say in this and that situation?" Then go within and find the answer. If it is not clear, take a piece of paper and pen, light a candle if you wish, and set your intention to find the answer inside of you. The master within is awake and alert at all times, forever waiting for your recognition.

- Let go of the third dimensional consciousness of separation, duality, polarity and drama in all its myriad forms. Stop believing in two powers, and giving your precious energy to the illusion of this 3D density. Allow yourself to set aside all that you have learned so far that has not given you the results you are yearning for. Be ready and willing to learn anew and have the courage to step into the unknown reality of Love and Magic. Recognize that Love is the only true power there is, and start living your life in that vibrational frequency from the inside out.

- Let go of all judgment and expectation about yourself and others, and how life should be unfolding for you. Allow yourself to perceive and embrace all the wonders and majesty of "YOU" in the splendor of your divinity, and accept the great adventure of letting it unfold and transform in front of your eyes, in deep joy and gratitude.

- Embrace the banner of humility and the sweet surrender to one's holy vows. If you don't know what they are, they are written within your very cells and DNA, as well as in many chambers of your Sacred Heart. Be willing to take the time to go within and investigate.

- Establish a conscious union with your I AM Presence and the fulfillment of your divine plan. The ascension is the unification, the merging into divine union with your magnificent I AM Presence. To embody this glorious aspect of yourself, make yourself familiar and intimate with that aspect of Self you want to merge with. How can you expect to ascend and unify with an aspect of Self that you have not spent the time to know and understand?

  When we ask people through channeling sessions what the ascension means to them, we are amazed at the answers we receive, such as changing dimension, being able to manifest everything, not having to be limited by money anymore, being able to teleport, and so on. Although these become the gifts and results of ascension, they are not its primary purpose. YOU, your level of understanding your divinity and becoming it brings it forth.

- Embrace the consciousness of harmlessness, by honoring the sanctity of all life sharing this planet with you and also the divine right of every person to live here as well.

- Release old programming running your life and all negative emotions stored in your conscious, unconscious and subconscious memories, including the balancing of all debts incurred towards life. You have already received many teachings on these topics.

- When individuals believe their debt to be light and they enter into the spirit of releasing it steadily into the sacred fire, they create a great release of joy that flows through their being. The feeling of joy within your consciousness has a tendency to create malleability in the coil of energy that keeps the records of the debts, relaxing tensions within the energetic coils, and freeing the individual to move on more quickly through all initiations with greater ease and grace.

- The attitudes that most assist anyone to move through the balancing of their shadow creation are twofold. First, adopt, as a way of life, each moment of the day "as an act of love" for yourself, for your fellowmen, for the planet, for other kingdoms sharing the planet with you and in gratitude for creation itself. And second, practicing the attitude of gratitude will assist you immensely.

- Nurture and expand a genuine desire for your ascension and immortality, embracing the willingness to walk the path unto the end! Unless you entertain a genuine desire for ascension and immortality, unless you are willing to shed the old ways of living in the third dimension that have kept you and humanity in pain, and walk the path shown to you by the Masters of Wisdom who have tread the way before you, you cannot become a true candidate for Ascension on the inner planes.

In seeking Ascension, the power of Love must become the fervent heat which will cause the elements of mortal creation to melt, and which will propel the candidate for Ascension into the great cosmic pool of immortal Love and Light.

Message from Serapis Bey

For those calling themselves seekers of truth who yearn for contact with the Hierarchy of Light and the Great White Brotherhood, it is required that you come directly under the guidance and the tutelage of the great master teachers. The path of mastery, achievement, freedom, victory and ascension can only be gained through the initiatic process. For all great masters who have ever ascended from this planet, or elsewhere, the Flame of Ascension has always remained a most important key which unlocks the door of immortality for every soul.

I have guarded, guided and stood within the Ascension Flame for a very long time, in order that there might be a way and means by which humanity, when through with their folly of the senses, could return to their Divine state. Since the "fall of man," if there had not been a guarding Brotherhood of the Ascension Flame, there would be no way back home for humanity. Have you ever pondered within the deepest recesses of your being what it would be like if there were no way back home?

To this end, many of us have remained prisoners of Love upon this temporary dark Star. The Lemurian Brotherhood of Light of Telos joined us in our vigil of Ascension for the planet. Together, we kept the Flame of Love and Light on behalf of mankind for thousands of years, until such a day when you had acquired enough spiritual maturity to partake in this planetary responsibility.

I am dedicated to see that you pass through the fires of purification and that you, who have applied for the opportunity of attaining the ascended status, will remain firm and vigilant in your commitment until that glorious victory becomes your reality. We are heart-friends of many ages.

Quote from Lord Jesus/Sananda

"Knowing the supreme glory of that hour, I can but urge each dear child of God to prepare for that glorious moment! When the hour comes and the summons from the Father of Light reaches your heart, you will also know the full and true purpose for human incarnations. It is to prepare your consciousness to become a Sun of Light within yourself, free of the wheel of birth and death, and a master of energy and vibration."

Those interested in visiting the Ascension Temples at Luxor and Telos are requested to bring back in their consciousness that rising, buoyant, joyous energy which is the activity of Ascension. This Flame will enter into the elemental substance of the inner bodies, as well as the physical form, and act as the "leaven in the loaf," when earnestly invoked. As the pure white Flame passes through the substance of the aspirant's bodies—physical, mental, emotional and etheric—it quickens the vibratory action of the atom, each electron moving more rapidly around its own central pole. This causes the throwing off of the impure, discordant substances around the electron, and quickens the rhythm of all the vehicles.

To ascend to the state of self-mastery, God wisdom, peace, harmony, perfect health, limitlessness, and ever-present supply, the candidate for the great gift of Ascension must learn to rely totally upon the Presence of God within the heart. The disciplines of the Ascension Brotherhood are designed to turn the consciousness from the outer world "inward," until, from within the heart center, the seat of your divinity, there is drawn forth and at will anything and everything which is required to manifest the fullness of your Divine Essence in physical manifestation. All must be purified and transformed through the ascending fires of that royal, dazzling, purifying Flame!

Codes of Conduct for a Disciple of the Holy Spirit

The Maha Chohan

1. Become conscious always of your aspiration to embody the full expression of Godhood, and devote all of your being and service to that end.

2. Learn the lessons of harmlessness—neither by word, nor thought, nor feeling will you ever inflict evil or harm upon any part of life. Know that action and physical violence will keep you in the realm of pain, suffering and mortality.

3. Stir not a brother's sea of emotion thoughtlessly or deliberately. Know that the storm in which you would place his spirit will sooner or later flow upon the banks of your own lifestream. Rather bring always tranquility, love, harmony and peace to all life.

4. Disassociate yourself from the personal and planetary delusion. Never allow yourself to love your little self more than the harmony of the universe. If you are right, there is no need to acclaim it. If you are wrong, pray for forgiveness.

5. Walk gently upon the Earth and through the universe, knowing that the body is a sacred temple, in which dwells the Holy Spirit, bringing peace and illumination to life everywhere. Keep your temple always in a respectful and purified manner, as befitting the habitation of the Spirit of Love and Truth. Respect and honor with gentle dignity all other temples, knowing that often within a crude exterior burns a great light.

6. In the presence of Nature, absorb the beauties and gifts of Her kingdoms in gentle gratitude. Do not desecrate Her by

vile thoughts, sounds or emotions, or by physical acts that despoil Her virgin beauty. Honor the Earth, "the Mother" that is hosting your evolutionary pathway.

7. Do not form nor offer opinions unless invited to do so, and then, only after prayer and silent invocation for guidance. Speak when God chooses to say something through you. At other times it is best to speak little, or to remain peacefully silent.

8. Let your heart sing a song of gratitude and joy unto God. Be grateful always for all that you have received and that you have in the now moment. Tap in to the River of Life, River of Love and Abundance that lies within the Sacred Heart.

9. In speech and action be gentle, but with the dignity that always accompanies the Presence of the living God that lives within the temple of your being. Constantly place all the faculties of your being and all the inner unfoldment of your nature at the feet of the God-power, endeavoring to manifest the perfection of compassion when meeting those in distress.

10. Let your word be spoken in gentleness, humility, and loving service. Do not allow the impression of humility to be mistaken for lethargy, for the servant of the Lord, like the sun in the heavens, is eternally vigilant and constantly outpouring the gifts of Love to those who open their hearts to receive them.

The Atomic Accelerator/Ascension Chair
A Tool for Creating a Chalice of Light

Greetings, beloveds, this is Adama with Master Saint Germain. I would like to talk to you about the atomic accelerator that many of you already know as the Ascension Chair used on the inner planes for several purposes. There are many of you who have studied the teachings of the former dispensations with Saint Germain, where this concept has been mentioned several times, but may not be fully understood. Allow us to give you now a greater understanding of this most wonderful tool, beloved ones, so that you can use it to assist yourselves and others on your pathway to Ascension.

As I speak, the energy of Master Saint Germain joins with me, and it is both of us collectively speaking to you, unifying our energies as one. In the light realms, the unity of consciousness is such that we can blend our energies and thoughts easily, which we very much enjoy doing.

The Atomic Accelerator, or the Ascension chair, is a gift to the Earth and to humanity from the heart of beloved Master Saint Germain. It is a tool to assist in raising the vibration of a candidate for Ascension. It contains the frequencies of the pure white Light of the Ascension Flame. It can also be used to raise one's vibration gradually and gently. When the dial is turned on full force, it will literally lift someone into the vibration of the electronic body for full, instant and permanent Ascension into the light realm and fifth dimensional consciousness.

In the past and now, many candidates on the inner planes, when ready for their earthly graduation, have received their full and majestic Ascension ceremony in the Light Realm, honored and supported by a large gathering of masters and beings from many dimensions, by sitting on one of these chairs. When the dial is turned on full force, all energies remaining in the records of the candidate, outpicturing less than pure Light and pure Love, are dissolved in the intensity of the Ascension frequency. Candidates are instantly transformed and reconnected consciously with the fullness of their Divine Essence, with all their spiritual gifts and attributes restored.

This is the true and permanent ceremony of divine union, beloveds! This is the great alchemical marriage with Self that so many of you long for. Although this is not the only way one can make their Ascension—there are indeed several other options—this one is the most commonly used now.

In order for one to receive this gift, one must be spiritually ready at all levels, or the results could be disastrous. You can trust that none of us would ever offer to do this with anyone who has not yet attained the full level of initiations required to receive such a blessing. There are a few of these chairs on this planet kept in various spiritual, fifth dimensional retreats of the Great White Brotherhood. We have one in Telos, Master Saint Germain has one at his retreat at Jackson Peak, Wyoming, and there are a couple at Luxor in Egypt. There is also one in the Himalayas and in a few other retreats.

Our channel, Aurelia, was directed by us several years ago to invite friends to her home once a month, to conduct a ritual Ascension ceremony for those desiring to deepen their commitment to this goal, to the spiritual hierarchy of the planet and to their I AM Presence. Each time Aurelia facilitated this ceremony with a group, a great number of us came to assist. Master Saint Germain always came with his portable Atomic Accelerator, which consists of a small etheric box, designed for that purpose which he positions beneath the chair in your dimension.

Each time, Saint Germain himself controls the intensity and velocity that each candidate can receive in order to raise their vibration to the next level, without significant discomfort or disturbance of the present level. This moveable accelerator box contains the same technology as a full version Atomic Accelerator Chair in the light realm. But the portable one is designed to be used for ceremonies performed in locations where surface people have chosen to do their Ascension work.

Aurelia has conducted these Ascension ceremonies since 1994, in her home while living in Montana. She has continued this service for the planet and for humanity ever since on a regular basis. She has performed this service of Light with every group that has come to Mount Shasta for initiatic journeys, and also in several other countries of the world during her travels abroad for conferences and workshops.

The Benefits and the Power of Building Momentum

We have noticed how wondrously powerful and beautiful the energies have become over the years, with each ritual Aurelia has facilitated, adding energy to the sum total of all past ceremonies. With great interest and gratitude, we observe that after many years of regular practice of this ritual, the Chalice of Light now created with each ceremony is building a huge momentum. The energies almost double in intensity and beauty each time this sacred ceremony is performed. It affects and helps not only the people participating in the group, but creates a web of Light touching almost the entire planet.

Many of you are not making the progress on your spiritual journey as rapidly as you would like or achieving the results you want in your mundane endeavors. This is mainly because you are not in the habit of creating enough momentum to achieve your goals. Building greater momentum is needed to gather enough energy in your world to create whatever you want.

Even the beings portraying the "shadow side" understand this principle very well, and they are far more vigilant in building their momentum of darkness than the People of Light have been in building their momentum of Light.

Your complacency is one of the main factors for the deep level of darkness, density and pain this whole planet has fallen into. Momentum of Light is what all of us who have become Masters have accumulated enough of in order to manifest whatever we want, at any time we desire it.

At first, in 1994, when Aurelia began to do her little ceremonies with four or five people, the Chalice of Light created with each ceremony was very small and not nearly as powerful as it is today. She continued to build her momentum, year by year, doing ceremonies each time she had enough people interested. She was unaware of its expanding impact.

With each ceremony, Master Saint Germain comes with his etheric atomic accelerator box, invisible to those not yet clairvoyant, and puts it beneath the chair designated and decorated for that purpose. In our realm, we consider it to be a physical box, made of fifth dimensional technology and certain types of crystals. It has dials that one can turn on and off, just like the technologies in your realm.

When the group is ready and the invocation of intention is made by the facilitator, Master Saint Germain turns on the atomic accelerator. What does it do? All around and beneath the chair, there is an emanation of Ascension frequency that begins radiating outward. The person sitting on the chair receives according to his level of evolution and capacity to receive.

The process is monitored carefully because the Ascension Flame energy emanating from the little box could literally make you become invisible if turned on too high. Be assured that until the time for the full glory of your Ascension comes, you will receive only safe increments each time you participate in these sacred ceremonies. As you evolve your consciousness, the Ascension Flame helps your purification process in greater measure each time, and assists in the raising of your vibration every time you set up your intention through this sacred ritual.

It is so beautiful when you do this, if you could only see it from our perspective. As you gather together, you assist and hold the energy for each other. Each person comes forth to sit on the chair to declare their desire and intention for Ascension before their friends and before their God. The candidate also declares the willingness to do whatever it takes to make this happen. As the candidate formulates his prayer, Master Saint Germain adjusts the dial of his accelerator to flood the forcefield with the level of Ascension frequency appropriate for that person in the now moment.

Each time you speak from the heart on the chair and set your intention for Ascension, you create an explosion of Love and Light that is most wondrous to behold. This is why, beloveds, when you hold these gatherings, there is always a large assembly of Light Beings from the many realms of this planet, many other planets and star systems who delight in seeing what you are doing. They wish to witness this wondrous explosion of Light created by members of surface humanity, always adding to your momentum of Light their love, support and comfort. *(End of transmission)*

Material Needed for an Ascension Ceremony

Preparation

- Before the ceremony, it is recommended *(but optional)* that one of the assistants spray the auric field of the participants with a sage mist or other kind of purifying essential oil infusion.
- It is highly recommended that the facilitator and the assistants wear white clothing to perform the ceremony. It is suggested, but not required, for the participants to also wear white clothing for the ceremony.
- Once the participants have arrived and are sitting *(on a chair or on the floor)* in the location where the ceremony is to take place, it is recommended that they remain silent and sit quietly in a meditative focus before the Ascension ceremony begins to prepare themselves and the forcefield for the blessing that is to take place.
- It is imperative that each participant considers this sacred activation to be an important step in his spiritual journey and seriously prepares the prayer request he is going to make while sitting on the Ascension Chair.

Chairs

- You will need a chair for the Ascension ceremony, draped with gold cloth or another elegant material.
- Two additional chairs in the front, one on each side of the Ascension chair, one for the facilitator and another one for the assistant *(if one is available)*.
- Provide chairs for the participants facing the Ascension Chair

Table

- Place a small table, preferably draped with gold cloth, between the ascension chair and the facilitator. On or around the table, put the following:
    - Flowers (optional)
    - Ascension crystal – Quartz or rose quartz for the candidate to hold near his heart while formulating his prayer
    - Tibetan bells, gong with mallet or other type of bell
    - Pictures of Master Saint Germain and Adama (placed in front, on the table, or other suitable place)
    - Golden cloth for small table and ascension chair
    - Water bottle on the floor for the facilitator
    - Box of Kleenex or other tissue paper near the ascension chair
    - Additional copies of the Candidature Request for Ascension

Other Material Needed

- Golden Liquid Light Activation: Sparkling apple juice or other liquid to be transubstantiated into an elixir of Light by Masters Saint Germain, Serapis Bey and Adama
- Small glass, small paper or plastic cups to hold the sparkling juice
- Trays to hold the cups with the liquid
- Contribution basket, as energy exchange, to balance the giving and receiving *(optional)*

How to Create Your Ceremony

Gather quietly in a semi-circle around the designated Ascension chair. Make sure to always leave a space of at least five to six feet between the chair and the circle of sitting participants. *(For the sake of clarity, we call "the candidate" the person who sits on the chair, and we use the pronoun "his" to indicate either gender.)*

It is advisable but not required to designate a particular place around or near the circle for the next candidate to get in line for the Ascension chair. As a candidate returns to his seat, another gets up and goes to the line. There should always be one person ready to go to the Ascension chair. This way, the flow remains more harmonious and uninterrupted.

When all preparations are in place and everyone is ready to begin, the facilitator rings Tibetan bells three times. Then the facilitator or a designated person begins the opening invocation. A gong can also be sounded before the opening invocation instead of the Tibetan bells.

Opening Invocation

In the name "I AM That I AM", I now call forth the Masters of Light and Wisdom from the fifth dimension and above, as we come together to the "Altar of the Ascension Flame". We now invite the participation of the members of the planetary hierarchy, Lord Sanat Kumara with Lady Venus, Lord Gautama Buddha, Lord Maitreya, Lord Sananda with Lady Nada, The Maha Chohan and the Chohans of the Seven Rays, Beloved El Morya, Lord Lanto, Master Kuthumi, Master Hilarion, Mother Mary, Quan Yin, and the Planetary Goddess, our beloved Mother Earth. We invite the presence of the Universal Judge. We also invite the presence of our Lemurian brothers and sisters of Telos and all beings of the

Earth's interior, as well as our brothers and sisters from the stars who wish to join us at this time. Last but not least, we invite Master Saint Germain, Adama and Lord Serapis Bey to officiate this ceremony of Ascension. We ask for Divine Grace, Mercy and Forgiveness, and that the maximum healing and peeling off layers of darkness be extended to each candidate. We also ask that our vibration frequency be raised permanently as much as each one's lifestream can allow. With this said, I now invite the first candidate to come forward.

Those gathered need to remain still while a candidate is making his prayer, to honor this sacred moment. Any movement needs to take place during the time someone returns to his seat, between candidates.

Each person comes forth to sit on the Ascension chair with a fully opened heart and offers his prayer request by stating aloud his intention, his goals for this life and his Ascension. Be willing to formulate the most honorable prayer your heart dictates or inspires you to do in the moment. This usually takes from three to five minutes.

When seated on the chair, the candidate picks up the Ascension prayer crystal on the table next to the chair. While making the prayer, the candidate holds the crystal close to his heart. When finished, remaining seated, he gives a sign of completion with the eyes, and the group sings three "AUMs" to assist the anchoring of this energy in the physical. The facilitator, or assistant, rings the Tibetan bells once prior to the singing of each of the three AUMs. Then the candidate puts back the crystal on the table or hands it to the facilitator, and returns to his seat. The next person comes forth. Candidates do not need to come in a specific order. There is always a natural flow created. The facilitator usually goes last, but this is not a rule.

Here is a sample prayer formulated on the Ascension Chair:

From the Lord God of my being, "I AM That I AM", I desire today to express and renew my deepest gratitude for this wondrous opportunity to present my request to be prepared for my ascension with my physical body in this lifetime, preferably around the year 2012 or before.

I ask the spiritual hierarchy of the planet and all my guides, angels and masters to infuse in me enough faith to continue on my pathway with great determination, even if I do not see, hear or feel you. I ask that my beingness be totally drenched in the purity of the Ascension Fire for total purification, so that only the purity of my divinity remains. I ask for the courage and the faith needed to maintain this goal until my Ascension has become my reality. I ask for forgiveness for all my errors of the past and choose from this day on to live my life with the Love and Wisdom of my Divine Essence. I ask for the full meaning of divine union to be revealed.

I ask for full support and assistance in creating my spiritual openings and the return of my spiritual gifts. I ask for divine union and a greater connection with all aspects of Self, particularly my beloved I AM Presence and my Higher Mental Body. I ask that the strength, the grace, the joy, the gentleness and the love be given to me to pass all tests and challenges presented to me, and to be taken to the next step and the next until I am totally ascended in the Light and Free.

I express my deepest gratitude for the blessings and the healing which grace my life each day and for my Ascension. With all my Love and Gratitude, I bow to the Light of my Divinity!

There is no right or wrong way of formulating your prayer request for Ascension. Simply let your heart speak and allow your true feelings to come forth and it will be perfect. Never compare your pathway and your prayers with others. You are all unique. Comparing creates the energy of self-doubt and is not constructive. During Ascension ceremonies, everyone benefits from the prayers of others as you are creating a group experience in oneness.

Golden Liquid Light Elixir

When everyone has come forward on the Ascension chair, prepare to receive a fifth-dimensional elixir of Light. Master Saint Germain, Serapis Bey and Adama invite you to drink an elixir which is charged with the frequency of the "Golden Liquid Light." While participants remain silent in a meditative state, there is a short pause while the facilitator with an assistant or two pour sparkling apple juice or other juice into small cups or containers and distribute them to each candidate.

The facilitator or assistant offers a short invocation asking that the liquid each person holds in their right hand be infused with the frequency of the Golden Liquid Light. The one making the invocation then pauses for a moment at the end of the invocation to allow the officiating Masters to transform the liquid to the frequency most appropriate for each candidate. When given the signal, each person SLOWLY drinks the liquid that has now become a "sacred alchemical elixir", expressing their deep gratitude for the gift and the rich blessings bestowed upon them.

Invocation

In the name "I AM That I AM", I now call for the beloveds Masters Saint Germain, Adama and Serapis Bey to transform, by the alchemy of Love, this liquid we hold in our hands into the vibration of pure Golden Liquid Light. We ask that this Golden Light frequency be adjusted to each one's needs according to what is most appropriate for each one. We give thanks for this Golden Liquid Light to infuse and transform every aspect of our beings into pure light essence, and for the many blessings we are receiving this day.

After a moment of silence and meditation in deep gratitude, the facilitator concludes the ceremony by ringing the Tibetan bells three times. Participants then come back to full consciousness and the silence can be broken.

Transmission from Adama and Master Saint Germain continued:

The elixirs created during Ascension activations are just as effective as the ones we give you on the inner plane. Some of you heard or read in one of the I AM books, around 1930, that David Lloyd drank the elixir given to him by Saint Germain on Mount Shasta. As soon as David drank it, his body began to lift and he gradually faded away until he completely disappeared. He ascended into the Realms of Light in front of a crowd, creating much wonderment for each one present. Know, beloved ones, that David LLoyd could have made his Ascension differently, but it was the choice his soul made in the inner plane to ascend in this wondrous manner, and it was granted. It happened this way because it was his time to ascend.

We could also charge the elixir for you in such a way that you could disappear, but that is not the plan for you right now. We are simply not going to do that, even if you ask! Not until it is your time, and believe us, several people have made that request. Sorry friends, for those who have requested this, it is imperative that you wait for your right timing.

There will come a time in the future when group Ascension will manifest, and in some cases, it will happen in front of others who will witness this. This time is not so far away. This will never take anyone who ascends by surprise. If this happens to you, it is because you are totally prepared and have fully consented to this type of Ascension.

When you hold your gatherings with the Atomic Accelerator, Master Saint Germain controls the exact amount of energy given to match the level of vibration each person can handle.

Some of you are hesitant or shy to speak from the heart openly in front of your brothers and sisters. Know, dear ones, in the light realms there are no secrets; everything is known. It is best that you start getting used to it now if you intend to come here. It will be easier later. Once you make it to the higher dimensions nothing can be hidden. It is a good practice to open your heart in front of your brothers and sisters and hold nothing back.

There is no shame in what you are doing and no one gets judged! It is so beautiful! It creates an explosion of Light each time, and your Light is amplified as you support each other, building a Momentum of Light on your "journey back to the stars."

We invite you now to start meeting in groups of all sizes in your cities, villages and countries, at least once a month, as brothers and sisters, to reinforce your desires and intentions for your spiritual goals. Allow a momentum to build with each ceremony and with each one's intentions. Imagine how powerful this can be! What you will be doing is creating little webs of Ascension Light everywhere on the planet that will gain greater and greater momentum as larger numbers of people do this.

This Momentum of Light will gain greater power as the energies created join together. This is the great Momentum of Light and Ascension Flame that is needed to propel this planet and all of humanity choosing to ascend in a great swirling tornado of Ascension Light that will dissolve all darkness and fully restore back every man, woman and child to the dignity of their divinity.

This is how darkness will be totally dispelled and swallowed up in a great victory of Light. But you have to do your part in your dimension, beloved children of our heart. It will not simply happen automatically without your contribution and participation, or by wishing it to be.

In Telos, we enjoy very much your ceremonies of Love and Intention. Be assured that I, Adama, Lord Serapis Bey and Master Saint Germain are with you as a team each time you perform your ceremonies, supporting and loving you until you create your Homecoming.

Adama - Do you wish to comment or do you have any questions on this subject?

Aurelia - This is the most incredible offering that you have given us about getting groups together around the world and experiencing levels of Ascension frequency through facilitating Ascension ceremonies and taking in spiritual elixirs. You are offering us a permanent increase of frequency through this beautiful ritual, is that correct?

Adama - We are, and you can do it as often as you wish. It is up to you if you want to use this as a tool to assist yourself on your pathway. It is a tool whose energies simply build up and increase as you unite together. Many people want to ascend, but they often forget to set their intention and are not always willing to put in the effort necessary to attain the fullness of their spiritual freedom.

When you get together and reinforce your intention, it becomes more powerful in your life. These gatherings can be created as wonderful ways to spend time together with like-minded people. You can share a meal together afterwards, if you wish. This is the Lemurian way, to do things together, without pomp or circumstance, simply being the gods and goddesses that we are. We invite you to do the same. Take advantage of these tools that are shown to you which assist you to raise your consciousness in very simple and pleasant ways. And so be it, beloved children of our heart. Be at peace and in love with yourself. Soon, we will meet face-to-face in the arms of Love.

Candidature Request for Ascension Before 2012

Commitment was originally taken on September 12, 2006 by a group of 22 French people during an initiatic journey at Ahnahmar's Garden on Mount Shasta.

In the name of Christ and of the Great "I AM" of my being, my Divine Essence,

- I now invite the presence of Prime Source, Creator of all universes as a witness.
- I also invite the presence of Sanat Kumara and of his beloved twin flame Lady Venus.
- I ask for the presence of the planetary Christ, Lord Maitreya and of Lord Sananda, as well as the presence of the Maha Chohan, who holds the office of the Holy Spirit for this planet.
- I invite the presence of the Chohan or guardian of each one of the seven rays, Masters El Morya, Lord Lanto, Paul the Venetian, Serapis Bey, Hilarion, Lord Sananda with Nada and Master Saint Germain.
- I invite the presence of the various aspects of the Divine Mother and her many representatives, such as the planetary Goddess in the person of our Earth Mother, the Lemurian Goddess represented by the sisterhood of Telos, Mother Mary and Quan Yin.
- I invite the presence of all our angels, guides and masters, known and unknown to us, who direct our destiny and assist our evolutionary process.
- Last, but not least, I also invite the presence of my beloved twin flame of the fifth dimension and beyond to be at my side.

I, (name)..., with full intention and with the fire of my heart flame, come here today to the altar of the Office of the Christ to place my candidature to receive full Ascension in harmony with the Earth's Ascension, accompanying Her during Her momentous graduation, or shortly thereafter.

I express my intention to walk the Earth as an Ascended Master with the full love, wisdom, power and majesty of an immortal being. I commit myself to do whatever work, on all levels, I need to fulfill all the prerequisites required to attain that level of unconditional love and evolution.

With an open and humble heart, I diligently commit myself to this goal in front of the spiritual hierarchy of this planet and those of the earth interior, including the king and queen of Telos, Adama, Ahnahmar, the Lemurian High Council of Telos and all our brothers and sisters of Telos, and all those who assist me in my spiritual journey towards Ascension.

I ask of the Beloveds Sanat Kumara, Lord Maitreya and Lord Sananda to receive all the assistance I need to attain my goal. May my request be heard in Heaven and on Earth! May all prerequisites be set in motion for the manifestation of my request! And so be it, beloved I AM!

______________________________ ______________

Sign your name Date

To receive a printed copy of this page and Master Saint Germain's message, contact us at aurelia@mslpublishing.com, and clearly state your request. We will be happy to e-mail it to you. Do not sign this request lightly; make sure that you are serious and firm with your solemn commitment to your Ascension.

Message from Master Saint Germain

Channeled by Denise Laberge as a result of this commitment

Peace be unto you, my brothers and sisters! I send into each one of your heart my Violet Flame Ray surrounded of gold, to assist you and to give you an extra level of strength to fulfill the solemn commitment you just made to the Creator, to your own "I AM Presence" and unto yourself.

It is for us of the Light Realm a great honor and privilege to see you all gathered here in this manner. It was for us a very great joy to witness the enthusiasm with which you have all accepted, without hesitation, to commit yourself to this great personal challenge. Know that the whole planet is most grateful for the engagement you just made.

The planetary Goddess, the Earth Mother, is now placing her hands upon your group, diffusing in each one of your hearts a golden-pink Ray of Light in order to bring her support, her love and her light to assist you directly in the commitment you just made. This commitment is not only personal, but also planetary, as it will serve the whole planet and humanity as well.

By your action, you have now just set in motion a great revolutionary movement in the Realms of Light and a great wave of awakening in the consciousness of humanity. In truth, each human being of this planet is linked to all others; you are all linked together.

In making this commitment verbally in this great celestial temple, you have been heard by all of Creation, and this, all the way to the Sacred Heart of the Creator. In order to thank you, an extraordinary assistance is now allocated to each of you. From this moment on, seven guides will remain with you permanently and will diligently assist you until the day of your Ascension. They will work with you relentlessly until your feet are solidly positioned on the last step of the Ascension golden stairway that will open for you the doors of the great Hall of Ascension.

Our hearts are filled with Joy and Light. Know that you are never alone. Be sure to ASK and ASK again and again the assistance of your guides. Ask them to join with the new guides that have just been assigned to you.

We bless you from our hearts. Know that our love for you is most pure and profound.

Prayer Section

Invocations to the Flame of Ascension for Personal and Planetary Healing and Transformation

Formulate these prayers once, three times, six times or nine times for each one, according to your inner guidance. Each time you repeat a prayer, you build a momentum of Light encoded in the prayer.

Prayer for Self-Love and for Ascension

From the Lord God of my Being, I AM That I AM, I decree:

I have Love for my journey into my Ascension.

I have Compassion for all physical and emotional pain I still need to heal.

I give thanks that I am now healing the past and resurrecting the new.

As a Master of Divine expression, walking the Earth, I now turn on the Light of my Divinity.

I now activate and transform my DNA to its fifth dimensional potential.

I now choose to completely heal and rejuvenate my physical body.

I choose to remain happy, harmonious and grateful.

I claim the mastery that is mine to manifest my freedom.

I allow my Divinity to manifest in a most wondrous way.

I give thanks that it is done according to God's Holy Will!

I call for shafts of Ascension Light to blaze through me daily and hourly. And so be it, beloved I AM!

(Repeat 3 times)

Ascension Affirmations

by Archangel Gabriel

I AM a fountain of Youth and Eternal Purity.

I AM the fullness of my Christ Victory.

I AM one with the Heart of God.

I AM the Purity of Love.

I AM the Purity of the Resurrection Flame.

I AM the Purity of the Healing Flame.

I AM the Purity of the Ascension Flame.

I AM the Purity of all my desires.

I AM the Purity of all my thoughts and feelings.

I AM the Purity of my intentions.

I AM the Purity of all my chakras.

I AM the Purity of Love in physical form.

I AM God in action in all I do.

I AM the fulfillment of my Ascension in the Light.

I claim my Freedom and Victory in the Light NOW!

(Repeat each affirmation 3 times)

Prayer for Personal Ascension

In the name of my beloved God-Presence "I AM," I ask to receive the initiations needed to qualify for Ascension. I call for a great cosmic shaft of Cosmic Purity Flame to remove from my mind, my thoughts, my feelings, my body and all subtle bodies, every vibration of human creation that is impure in substance and less than my Divine Perfection in God.

May the Flame of Purity transmute from my world
all remaining negative energies!
May the Love of Christ expand in me
through the power of the Ascension Flame!
May the Resurrection Flame awaken the memories
of my divine blueprint,
So that I can be free forever from all discord
I have ever created!

I affirm that I AM Purity in action.
I AM God's Purity established within mind, body and soul.
Let me also invoke Purity for every part of Life on Earth.
Let me invoke Purity for my family, my friends and for the
whole family of God, all Kingdoms and the Earth.
And so it is, beloved I AM!

(Repeat the last 2 paragraphs 3 times)

I Accept the Gift of My Ascension Now!

Beloved Heavenly Father/Mother God and my own God-Presence I AM, within and above me, I greet you and send you my purest divine love and gratitude. I thank you for the gift of Life and ask for the gift of my Ascension in the Realm of Light and Love. It is my desire and intention to fulfill my Divine Plan on Earth and assist the Earth and my fellowmen to do likewise.

I ask that you prepare my soul for my Ascension in this life and put before me all the lessons I need to learn to successfully pass all levels of the seven Sacred Initiations to qualify for my Ascension. I ask for the purification process necessary to make this happen be shown to me daily. I also ask that my purification unfold with love, ease, grace, wisdom and gentleness. With the deepest Love, Humility and Surrender, I now make this request.

With the deepest Love, Humility, Gratitude and Surrender,
I open myself to receive the gift of my Ascension.

With the deepest Love, Humility, Gratitude and Surrender,
I declare that as a Child of God, I am worthy of my Ascension.

With the deepest Love, Humility, Gratitude and Surrender,
I accept my Ascension now and I fully accept my Divinity.

With the deepest Love, Humility, Gratitude and Surrender,
I accept all the gifts that are mine to receive as a Unified Being!

I give thanks for the gift of my Ascension in this life!
And so be it, beloved I AM!

Prayer for Transformation and Ascension

My beloved I AM Presence, I acknowledge you as the Source of my being and life. I ask for the Divine Plan for my life and my Holy Purpose on Earth to be made manifest now. Please shine your Love and your Light into my heart and into all my chakras, into my mind, my feelings and my physical body.

I hold myself willing and ready to receive more of Thy Light and Thy Presence so that I may express and expand my consciousness through Thy Christ Love and Wisdom. I ask that you monitor my heart and feeling world to receive daily and in all matters of my life the Wisdom and Guidance that will quickly take me, with ease and grace, through the Seven Temples of the path of initiation to receive the gift of my Ascension as soon as I meet all requirements.

Charge all conditions and activities of my physical life with your Sacred Fire, Love, Purity, Beauty, Grace, Divine Perfection and with all the God-attributes of the Seven Sacred Flames. Reveal your Divine Will to me daily and release in me the Illumination Ray of the Mind of God. Infuse in me the Healing Power of your Eternal Presence. And so be it, beloved I AM!

Prayer for Purity

In the name of my beloved victorious God-Presence I AM, I affirm that I Am worthy of thy Purity. I call for a great cosmic shaft of Cosmic Purity Flame to remove from my mind, my thoughts, my feelings and my body, every vibration of human creation that is impure in substance and that is less than my Perfection in God.

Replace it all with the fullness of the Mind of Christ. Manifest within me the power of the Resurrection and the Ascension Flames so that, by the power of Purity's Ray, I might be free from all discord I have ever created and all discord that has ever been directed against me and the Light for which I stand.

I Am Purity in action. I Am God's Purity established within my soul, my mind and my body. Let me also invoke Purity for every part of life on Earth, for my family, my friends, the whole family of God, all Kingdoms and the Earth Mother. And so it is, beloved I AM!

(Repeat the last 2 paragraphs 3 times)

Invocation to the Golden Pink Ray

In the name of the victorious Presence of God I AM, I call to the heart of beloved Serapis Bey and the Brotherhood of the Ascension Flame at Luxor, Beloved Saint Germain, Beloved Jesus/Sananda, Beloved Sanat Kumara and Lady Venus, Seven Mighty Elohim and Seven Beloved Archangels, and the Seven Chohans of the Rays. I invoke the Golden Pink Ray from the Heart of God to enfold my four main body systems and all my other subtle bodies and I say:

Golden Pink Light from the Heart of God *(3 times)*
Infuse my form with thy dazzling Golden Pink Radiance.
Saturate me with the Golden Pink Light from above
Saturate me with the pure-white Ascension Flame
Raise me up into Thy Eternal Glory.
Resurrect my entire consciousness being and world.
Illumine and charge me with the Light of Cosmic Love
For the Victory of my Ascension and the Victory
Of my Eternal Freedom in the Light.
As I call this for myself and for the Earth, I also call this
For every man, woman and child on this planet.
And so it is, beloved I AM!

(Repeat the last 12 lines 3 times)

Invocation to the Cosmic Ascension Light

Beloved Glorious I AM Presence, Light of my soul, may the Light of Cosmic Ascension and Divine Love be poured within my soul and into the Earth like the Light of a thousand Suns to permeate the Earth and to saturate Her people and Her many kingdoms.

May all negativity, illusion and karma be transmuted by this Cosmic Ascension Light of God that never fails! May the Great Golden Age of enlightenment, love, peace, brotherhood and prosperity for all be established now upon our dear planet by the action of this Great Ascension Light! By the authority of my Beloved I AM Presence, the Light of the Father/Mother God, and by the authority of the entire Spirit of the Great White Brotherhood I affirm:

As a Son of God, I now declare that I AM an authority on Earth. I AM calling for the action of the Light of a thousand suns to be released now on this beloved planet for the immediate transformation of Earth into the "Shining Star" that is Her destiny and for the raising up of humanity into their Eternal Freedom in the Realms of Light and Divine Perfection. I request that the Light that is needed to manifest the Kingdom of God on Earth, as it is in Heaven, be released now without limit until all is ascended in the Light and Free. And so it is, beloved I AM!

(Repeat three times or as many times as you feel guided to. You are building a greater momentum of Light each time you repeat this and all prayers.)

Seal the Earth with Ascension Fire

Beloved Mighty Victorious Presence of God of my Being, I AM, and of all Humanity, Beloved Legions of the Ascension Flame, Angels of Purity and Victory, Brotherhoods of the Ascension Fire at Luxor and Telos, and the entire Spirit of the Great White Brotherhood, I decree:

SEAL! SEAL! SEAL our dear Earth, Her atmosphere, all of Her governments, Her people and Her many kingdoms, in OCEANS and WAVES of UNLIMITED MIGHTY ASCENSION FLAME! Let the Fiery Essence of the Ascension Flame penetrate and saturate every man, woman and child on this planet, every animal, every mountain, every ocean, river and lake, every tree, blade of grass, every flower, lifting and raising all life upon Earth out of human negativity into the glorious frequency of the Christ Light and the Perfection of the Ascended State!

Sustain that vibration forever! Infuse the Ascension Flame and the Fire of Divine Love into every particle of Life upon this planet and its evolution. Allow us all to return to the House of our Father/Mother God from whence we came, forever to remain in the Eternal Victory of God's Divine Plan Fulfilled! I give Thanks that this is done, for I have made this call in God's most holy name I AM! And so be it, beloved I AM!

(Repeat the last 2 paragraphs 3 times)

Flood the Earth with Radiant Ascension Flame

In the name of the victorious Presence of God, I AM, I call to the Masters of Light from the entire spirit of the Great White Brotherhood, Beloved Goddess of Purity, Beloved Serapis Bey, and the Brotherhood of the Ascension Flame at Luxor and Telos, Beloved Queen of Light and Beloved Angels of the Radiant Ascension Flame.

Flood every particle of life on Earth with oceans and oceans of Violet Fire and Ascension Flame. Purify, illumine and raise the consciousness of all life and all kingdoms evolving here. Let thy Flame blaze, illumine and expand like the Light of a thousand suns. Purify our minds, memories and feeling world from all blockages and negativity. Purify our bodies from all diseases and weaknesses. Flood our world with the pure snow-white radiance of the Ascension Flame purity! Saturate and purify until we become crystal clear, transforming all we contact with the Radiant Light of the Ascension Flame.

> Blaze the Radiant Ascension Flame through us. *(3 times)*
> Flood and saturate the Earth with oceans of Violet Flame.
> Flood the Earth with the Radiance of the Ascension Fire.
> Cut us free to be with Thee in the Realms of Eternal Freedom
> And Infinite Perfection now and forever!
> And so be it, beloved I AM!

(Repeat the last 6 lines 3 or 6 times)

The Time is Now!

The time is now to turn on the Light of my Divinity.

I now open myself to the River of Love
that lies within my heart. Let Love flow endlessly!

I now open myself to the River of Life
that lies within my heart. Let Life flow endlessly!

I now open myself to the River of Light
that lies within my heart. Let Light flow endlessly!

I now open myself to the River of Peace
that lies within my heart. Let Peace flow endlessly!

I now open myself to the River of Joy
that lies within my heart. Let Joy flow endlessly!

I now open myself to the River of Abundance
that lies within my heart. Let Abundance flow endlessly,
ready to project infinite Grace and Gifts upon my daily Life,
now and forever!

I now open myself to the River of Violet Flame
that will purify me through my Ascension.

Hear, Oh Universe, I am Grateful!

(Repeat 3 times)

Song of Thanksgiving

My beloved I AM Presence,
Grateful am I now for thee!
Flooding forth life's perfect essence,
Setting all the earth now free!
Let us see thyself now clearly,
Oh—rend now the human veil.
Bless the Masters we love dearly,
By their love, God does prevail!
Thank you for the air we're breathing,
Thanks for earth and sea and sky,
Thank you for the many blessings
Men so thoughtlessly pass by.
Thank you for a heart that's beating,
Thanks for home and comforts too,
Thanks for perfect sight and hearing,
All through love that flows from you!
Thank you for the blessed sunshine
Filling all our worlds with cheer,
Thank you for the elementals,
And the friends we hold so dear.

Thank you for love's great forgiveness,
Thanks for loving mercy, too,
Thanks for God's great gift of healing,
Oh—thanks for ALL YOU do!
Bless America "THE FREE,"
Lift her people out of bondage,
Raise their consciousness to thee.
Hold them in the heart of freedom,
Seal them in his Violet flame,
Purify their homes and families
Through the love of Saint Germain!
My beloved I AM Presence,
Grateful am I now for thee,
Take my body, mind and spirit,
Take the heart and soul of me.
Make of me thy perfect chalice,
Messenger of love and peace,
By the light of God,
Give us Ascension's sweet release.
(Author unknown)

About Aurelia Louise Jones

Aurelia Louise Jones was born in Montreal in a French Canadian family in the early 1940's. She graduated as a nurse in the early part of her working career, and worked as a Health Counselor most of her adult life, as a naturopath and a homeopath, using various holistic modalities. She moved to the USA in 1989.

Under the sponsorship of the Brotherhood of Light and the order of Melchizedek, she was ordained as a minister in 1998. She devotes most of her time to her spiritual ministry ever since. In her role as a spiritual teacher of higher consciousness, her main focus is to awaken the consciousness of humanity to the spiritual truths leading to Ascension.

In 1997, while living in Montana, she received direct guidance from Adama and the Lemurian Council of Light of Telos to move to Mount Shasta in preparation for the fulfillment of her work with them, which has become the major expression of her life. She moved to Mount Shasta one year later in June 1998.

She was the founder and owner of Mount Shasta Light Publishing and The Lemurian Connection Network. At the request of Lady Quan Yin, Aurelia Louise channeled through her cat Angelo a touching message from the animal kingdom, now in booklet form called: *"Angelo's Message to the World."* Angelo was her favorite cat who incarnated to be with her in order to bring his message on behalf of the animal kingdom.

She published the Telos books series, Volume 1,2,& 3, and now *"The Seven Sacred Flames,"* bringing the Lemurian teachings to the surface population. The Telos series publications are published in many countries and in several languages.

On July 12th, 2009, Aurelia Louise Jones made her transition, leaving us a rich legacy of transformational tools, inspiring us to live from our hearts and fully embrace the Lemurian way of life. Through her channeling of Adama and the Masters of Light, Aurelia's teachings bring forth invaluable "food for thought" which is timeless in its nature. There has never been a more appropriate time than the present moment to attune our hearts to Love, Compassion and above all, Ascension. These are the key elements in Aurelia's heartfelt message from Adama and our Telosian family and all the Ascended Masters of Light and Love. This will set us free, moving us into the next vibrational frequencies, the fifth dimension and beyond.

Aurelia's dream and desire was to awaken humanity during this monumental time of change, to increase the Lemurian Connection around the world and to spread the Light of Adama's message through her books about Telos and the Lemurian way of living. She had great love and a deep gratitude for the planet, beloved Mother Earth, humanity and especially the animals. Her dedication was unwavering and this mission was ever present the last 10 years of her life.

Aurelia's books have touched the lives of thousands of people all over the world. Telos communities have been created in many countries through sheer inspiration to live from the Lemurian Heart. As people embrace the Telos books, study groups are forming to support one another on their sacred spiritual journey. We are grateful to have the Telos books, the teachings and channelings of Aurelia Louise Jones awaken us to our Lemurian heritage.

Mt. Shasta Light Publishing is dedicated to continuing Aurelia's heartfelt mission, spreading the Lemurian teachings and opening our hearts to Ascension. Her work continues to be distributed throughout the world.

Mount Shasta Light Publishing Publications

The Seven Sacred Flames (hardcover) $44.00

The Seven Sacred Flames (paperback) $33.00

Seven Flames Prayer Booklet $7.00

Ascension Activation Booklet $7.00

Seven Sacred Flames Card Deck $16.00

Telos Book Series Card Deck $16.00

Telos – Volume 1 "Revelations of the New Lemuria" $18.00

Telos – Volume 2 "Messages for the Enlightenment of a Humanity in Transformation" $18.00

Telos – Volume 3 "Protocols of the Fifth Dimension" $20.00

The Effects of Recreational Drugs on Spiritual Development... $4.00

Angelo's Message – "Angelo, the Angel Cat Speaks to all People on this Planet regarding the Treatment of Animals by Humanity"............................. $8.00

Spanish:

Las Siete Llamas Sagradas $24.00

Oraciones de las Siete Llamas Sagradas $7.00

La Llama de la Ascensión de Purificación e Inmortalidad $7.00

Telos – Libro 1 "Revelaciones de la Nueva Lemuria" $18.00

These publications can be purchased:

- Directly from us by phone or mail to P.O. mailing address
- From our secure shopping cart on our web site: https://www.mslpublishing.com
- Book stores through New Leaf book distributing

Mount Shasta Light Publishing
P.O. Box 1509, Mount Shasta, CA 96067-1509
Phone: 530-926-4599
(If no answer, leave a message)

Telos and Lemurian Connection Associations

Telos Worldwide Foundation (Canada)
Telos Australia
Telos Brazil
Telos Europe
Telos France
Telos Israel
Telos Ivory Coast
Telos Japan
Telos Latinoamerica
Telos UK
Telos USA

For each country's website go to
Telos-The Lemurian Connection
www.lemurianconnection.com

Canadian Distributors:
Quanta Books Distributing
3251 Kennedy Road, Unit 20
Toronto, Ontario, MIV-2J0 CANADA
Phone: 1-888-436-7962 or 416-410-9411
quantamail@quanta.ca
www.quanta.ca

For Publishers in other languages
please check our website:
www.mslpublishing.com